DEXTER v MERTON

Paul Blum

RISING★STARS

Rising Stars UK Ltd.
22 Grafton Street, London W1S 4EX
www.risingstars-uk.com

nasen

NASEN House, 4/5 Amber Business Village, Amber Close,
Amington, Tamworth, Staffordshire B77 4RP

Published 2008

Cover design: pentacorbig
Illustrator: Chris King, Illustration Ltd.
Text design and typesetting: pentacorbig
Publisher: Gill Budgell
Editor: Catherine Baker
Editorial project management: Margot O'Keeffe
Editorial consultant: Lorraine Petersen
Photos: Alamy

British Library Cataloguing in Publication Data.
A CIP record for this book is available from the British Library.

ISBN: 978-1-84680-460-1

Printed by Craft Print International Limited, Singapore

Contents

The Crash

- The Crash happened in 2021. Alien space ships crash landed on Earth.

- After The Crash, the Earth became very cold and dark.

- Now the aliens rule the world.

- The aliens have changed shape so they look like people.

- People call the aliens The Enemy.

Life after the Crash

- People are afraid.

- They do not know who is an Enemy and who is a friend.

The Firm

- The Firm keeps order on the streets.

- The Firm keeps people safe from Enemy attacks.

About Matt Merton

Matt Merton works for The Firm. He often works with Dexter. Their job is to find and kill The Enemy. They use Truth Sticks to do this.

But Matt has problems.

Matt has lost his memory. He cannot answer some big questions.

- Where has Jane, his girlfriend, gone?

- How did he get his job with The Firm?

Matt thinks The Firm is on the side of good. But is it?

chapter 1

A loud bang shook the coffee bar.

'What's that, Matt?' asked Sam.

'I don't know, Sam, but I'll find out.

'I'll take my coffee to go,' said Matt.

'You're late,' said Dexter.

'I was getting a coffee,' said Matt.
'So where are we going today?'

'We are going to the woods. The Enemy are hiding there.

They are building bombs,' said Dexter.

They drove fast.

They drove deep into the woods.

chapter 2

Suddenly, a loud bang shook the car.

The windows cracked. The power died.

'No signal. We have to get out.
We have to walk,' said Matt.

Suddenly, a light shone into the car.
A woman and a girl looked in.

'I work for The Firm. Put up your hands,'
said Dexter.

'We have done nothing wrong,' said the woman.

'Stand to the side,' Dexter told the girl.
He shone the Truth Stick in her eyes.

chapter 3

'You must follow us,' said the woman.

'It's a trap, Matt,' said Dexter.

'The Enemy know you are here. They will kill you,' said the woman.

Matt could see they did not have 'the look'.
They were not The Enemy.

But Dexter kept on shining the Truth Stick in their eyes.

'They are lying. They must die,' he said.

Matt pulled Dexter away from the girl.

'Let her go. She is one of us,' he said.

'This way,' said the woman.

She led them through the woods.

She led them through the shadows.

'This tunnel will take you back to the city' said the woman.

'Will you be safe?' asked Matt.

They were all in danger now.

'Don't worry about us, ' she said. 'You must go now!'

'Just run. Don't look back,' said the woman.

'Tell The Firm that The Enemy are making another bomb. A very big bomb. It will kill lots of people,' she said.

'How can we stop them?' asked Matt.

'The Enemy will put the bomb in a plane. You
must shoot it down before it crashes into the city,'
the woman said.

chapter 4

Two days later a plane flew over the city.

An even louder bang shook the coffee bar.

This time Matt knew what it was. The Firm had
shot down the plane.

Matt thought about the woman and girl.
They had saved him and the city. For now…

AUTHOR NAME
Paul Blum

JOB
Teacher

LAST KNOWN LOCATION
North London, England

NOTES
Before The Crash taught in Inner-city London
schools. Writer of series of books called
The Extraordinary Files. Believed to be in
hiding from The Firm. Wanted for questioning.
Seems to know more about The Enemy than
he should ...